D1237882

Amazing Arctic Explorer
MATTHEW HENSON

Mary Dodson Wade

Enslow Elementary

an imprint of

Enslow Publishers, Inc.

40 Industrial Road
Box 398
Berkeley Heights, NJ 07922
USA

http://www.enslow.com

Enslow Elementary, an imprint of Enslow Publishers, Inc.
Enslow Elementary® is a registered trademark of Enslow Publishers, Inc.

Library of Congress Cataloging-in-Publication Data

Wade, Mary Dodson.
    Amazing arctic explorer Matthew Henson / Mary Dodson Wade.
       p. cm. — (Amazing Americans)
    Includes index.
    Summary: "Readers will find out about Matthew Henson's life and his quest to reach
the North Pole with Robert Peary"—Provided by publisher.
    ISBN-13: 978-0-7660-3286-6
    ISBN-10: 0-7660-3286-8
    1. Henson, Matthew Alexander, 1866-1955—Juvenile literature. 2. African American explorers—
Biography—Juvenile literature. 3. North Pole—Discovery and exploration—Juvenile literature.
    I. Title.
    G635.H4W33 2009
    910.92—dc22
    [B]
                      2008024894

Printed in the United States of America

10 9 8 7 6 5 4 3 2 1

Illustration Credits: AP, p. 19; Everett Collection, p. 16; Library of Congress, Prints and Photographs Division, pp. 4, 7, 11, 15; National Archives, p. 8; Shutterstock, p. 12.

Cover Illustration: Library of Congress, Prints and Photographs Division (Matthew Henson); © Shutterstock

CONTENTS

CHAPTER 1

Growing Up

Matthew Henson was born in 1866 on a farm in Maryland. When he was young, both of his parents died. He left his home to find work on a ship. Years later, he became the first African American to reach the North Pole.

◄ Matthew Henson explored the Arctic with Robert Peary.

Matthew was only 12 when he went to sea. He cleaned cabins and helped the cook. The captain taught Matthew how to read and write. He even taught him how to navigate using stars. Then the ship captain died. Matthew went back to Washington, D.C. He got a job in a store.

Matthew Henson sailed out of shipyards like this one. ▶

Matt
Henson

CHAPTER 2

Working with Peary

One day, Robert Peary came into the store. He was going to Central America to explore. The store owner said Henson would be a good helper.

For more than a year Henson worked with Peary. Henson knew how to build things from wood. He could fix machines. He even helped plan where to put roads.

◄ Matthew Henson, in the back, worked with Peary in Central America.

Peary wanted to be the first man to get to the North Pole. He knew Henson was strong and smart. He asked him to join the crew of his ship.

He knew Henson could do things that would be helpful on the journey. He asked Henson to join his crew. They boarded the ship and set sail for the cold Arctic.

Robert Peary on the deck of a ship. He was trying ▶
to reach the North Pole.

NORTH POLE

CHAPTER 3

To the North Pole!

The ship landed near an Inuit village. When the people saw Henson's dark skin, they thought he was Inuit too. Henson learned to speak their language. He became a good dog sled driver. He helped Peary make maps.

◀ Henson and Peary tried to reach the North Pole many times.

Henson and Peary would not make it to the North Pole on this trip. They tried six more times, but storms and ice always stopped them.

Finally, on April 6, 1909, Henson and Peary got to the North Pole. It had taken them eighteen years to get there.

Matthew Henson learned how to drive a dog sled. ▶

Awards

Robert Peary became a famous man. Because Henson was African American, nobody talked about what he had done. It took many years before he was given any awards.

◀ **Peary took a picture of Henson and the four Inuit who reached the North Pole with him.**

Matthew Henson was 89 years old when he died on March 9th, 1955. Today, he is remembered as one of the world's greatest explorers. He never gave up on his goal of reaching the North Pole.

In 1942, Matthew Henson received a gold medal ▶ from the Geographic Society of Chicago.

SOMETHING TO THINK ABOUT

It was many years before Matthew Henson became famous. The U.S. Navy gave him a medal. A TV movie called "Glory & Honor" was made about him. A postage stamp honored him.

What do you think would be the best way to honor him?

Matthew Henson wrote a book about going to the North Pole. In it, he said, "The lure of the Arctic is tugging at my heart." The word *lure* means something that pulls you toward it.

What place is your favorite place? Why do you like to go there?

TIMELINE

1866—Born in southern Maryland.

1887—In Central America with Robert Peary.

1891–1892—First trip to the Arctic.

1893–1895—Second trip to the Arctic.

1896—Third trip to the Arctic.

1897—Fourth trip to the Arctic.

1898–1902—Fifth trip to the Arctic.

1905–1906—Sixth trip to the Arctic.

1908–1909—Reached the North Pole on April 6, 1909.

1955—March 9, died in New York City.

★Words to Know

Arctic—The part of the world around the North Pole.

Central America—The land between North America and South America.

explorer—Someone who travels into unknown areas.

Inuit—A group of people who live in the Arctic.

navigate—To find the course or location of a ship.

 Learn More

Books

Armentrout, David and Patricia Armentrout. *Matthew Henson.* Vero Beach, FL: Rourke Publishing, 2003.

Honea, B. A. *Matthew Henson.* Mankato, MN: Capstone Press, 2006.

Weidt, Maryann N. *Matthew Henson.* Minneapolis, MN: Lerner Publishing, 2002.

Internet Addresses

"Matthew Henson, Arctic Explorer"
http://www.enchantedlearning.com/explorers/page/h/henson.shtml

INDEX